DEAR LORD

Samantha Nacole

DEAR LORD.

Please direct all copyright inquiries to:

B.O.Y. Publications, Inc.
c/o Author Copyrights
P.O. Box 262
Lowell, NC 28098
betonyourselfent.com

Paperback ISBN: 978-1-955605-78-6

Cover and Interior Design: B.O.Y. Enterprises, Inc.

Printed in the United States.

DEDICATION

I dedicate this prayer journal to my four blessings who call me Mom; Jay Jay, My'Angel, Aurellia, and Jr for always seeing the best in me. I love you all beyond words.

To My Blessed and Highly Favored Reader,

The BEST tool we are blessed to have is prayer! I encourage you to use it until you can't use it anymore. If you're wondering how to pray.....just be YOU. The same way you talk in your everyday life is the same way you can talk to God. Don't ever think you have to be perfect because that will set you up for failure every time. If perfection is what we all had, there wouldn't have been any reason for Jesus to sacrifice His own life. On the days you can't begin to find words, ask God to listen to your heart. He knows and can understand every type of language known to man. All He wants is to hear from you, day and night. You are His child, and He loves you unconditionally. Make prayer a habit. Welcome the Holy Spirit into your life every day for guidance.

Sincerely,

Samantha

INTRODUCTION

Truth be told, I used to practice prayers in my head, and THEN try to present them to God. For whatever reason, I thought I'm supposed to present them a certain way or with a certain posture. I have asked believers, "How do I pray? What am I supposed to say?" The answer was always the same: "Just like you're talking to me. " Do what??!! Eventually, I tried it, and I tried it some more. I began asking God to teach me how to pray. Now, at any given moment, I'll pray BOLDLY. And guess what? I am completely myself. There are days I pray that He listens to my heart.

Those are the days when my tears do the talking for me, and I rest in His arms while He strengthens me. I don't give up. Get so comfortable with God that you know all the ways to get your prayers to Him. As you read the prayers, I have written in this prayer journal, invite Holy Spirit to guide you as you write your own prayers. Remember, your prayers don't have to sound like mine or anyone else's. God just wants to hear you come to Him as your authentic self!

Let's Pray!

Dear Lord,

Please soften my heart. Help me to forgive as quickly as you forgive. Teach me how to show mercy as you have shown me more times than I deserve. Take the taste of bitterness and hatred out of my mouth. You require us to love EVERYONE. Allow my flesh to bow down and my spirit to bring glory to your name. The gift of love you have given so freely, I want it to pour out no matter what situation I am faced with. Teach me how to pray for my enemies. Tame my tongue so I won't be in a battle of word for word. My flesh is weak, but You God can strengthen me. In Jesus' name, amen!

Prayer

Date: _____

Dear Lord,

I don't believe we run into people by chance. So when I meet someone new, allow your words to flow like honey. I am willing to be used by You, Lord. Let me be someone they can relate to so I can tell my testimony, and they see You and Your mighty works in me; more of You and less of me always. Please guide me in this world to the people who need a savior and may not even realize it. When they see me, they see you. I am your disciple. Lord, use me.

Amen

Prayer

Date: _____

Dear Lord,

Thank You for the unexpected rain as a reminder of who's STILL in control. Oftentimes, we walk around like it's "us" that made it happen. When in all reality YOU are The One who's always in control of everything. And for that Lord, I thank you for new grace and new mercy. Even with high water, you spared my life one more time. There's a hunger for growth, and we know everything needs water to grow. Rain on every area of my life that You are calling for me to grow. Amen

Prayer

Date: _____

Dear Lord,

I thank you for the future deliverance of my family members, who are trying to fight off their addiction. Break their chains, take the taste of it out of their mouths. Give them a hunger for You, Lord. Addictions can not be overcome alone. We need You. Fill the room with testimonies that stir up hope for others. Allow my family to be the example to show that it can be done. No more drugs, no more alcohol, no more needles, no more pills, but continual praise and glory for forgiveness and another chance.

Amen

Prayer

Date: _____

Dear Lord,

It's not the belief that I lack so much, but I need help with my unbelief that sits in the back of my mind. Taking up unnecessary space. I know it's the enemy trying to distract me, but it is You, Lord who holds all power. Help me to take you out of this box because I know You are too big and very limitless. So I am trusting you with my every thought. Please fill it with your words and your way.

Amen

Prayer

Date: _____

Dear Lord,

Today's thoughts are yesterdays events, and they are hitting me extra heavy. I need a little more grace and a little more mercy, please. I don't want to be robbed of the joys of this day. I don't want to be stuck in the past, and I don't want to worry about my tomorrow because you said to let tomorrow worry about itself. Turn yesterday's problem loose in Jesus' name.

Amen

Prayer

Date: _____

Dear Lord,

I thank You for waking me up with a song of praise in my heart for you. I will live today with purpose. Purposeful joy. Purposeful peace. Purposeful praise. Purposeful happiness. When troubles come, I will sing Your praises. I will be more mindful of all the blessings You've given today. I will see all the good you have done.

Amen

Prayer

Date: _____

Dear Lord,

As I read your Word, show me what it means. Help me to live it, keep your commandments, and love like You love. Help me to retain it so that when trials and tribulations are pouring in every way, I'll speak them with authority. Your words will be lived every day. I don't want to read just to say I've read. I want to apply it to my life daily. I want it to pour out. I want it to become a habit. Lord, I thank You in advance.

Amen

Prayer

Date: _____

_____
_____
_____
_____
_____
_____
_____
_____
_____
_____
_____
_____
_____
_____
_____
_____
_____
_____
_____
_____
_____
_____
_____

Dear Lord,

I'm coming to you as boldly as I know how to ask for forgiveness for my impure thoughts and behaviors. It's never my intention to live in the flesh, but mine does get weak from time to time. I know I can overcome them, but only if you deliver me. Direct my eyes to You, God. The taste of bitterness consumes me. Some days, it has me in a chokehold. Cast it all out in the sea of forgetfulness to return no more.

Amen

Prayer

Date: _____

_____
_____
_____
_____
_____
_____
_____
_____
_____
_____
_____
_____
_____
_____
_____
_____
_____
_____
_____
_____
_____
_____
_____
_____
_____

Dear Lord,

I have allowed the enemy to rob me blind. He took my peace of mind, the joy I once felt, and my self-love has been compromised. All things that once were are no longer. How can I allow something that was given to me to be taken in the blink of an eye? Father God, I ask that You change this narrative. Wash me clean, and make me whole again. Allow me back in Your presence, Your light O God, I pray.

Amen

Prayer

Date: _____

Dear Lord,

The spiritual gifts you have blessed me with, I am beyond grateful for. Teach me how to use them for Your glory. Don't ever let me use them for person gain. When I stray, Lord, put me back on track immediately. Protect my gifts, Lord. I know the enemy will try to destroy anything that brings glory to Your name. Don't let me be taken off guard. Pour out Your discernment so I can recognize it a mile away.

Amen

Prayer

Date: _____

_____
_____
_____
_____
_____
_____
_____
_____
_____
_____
_____
_____
_____
_____
_____
_____
_____
_____
_____
_____
_____
_____
_____
_____
_____
_____

Dear Lord,

I have to be honest with you because I am aware that You already know my thoughts before I do. The situation I'm going through has me fearful. Yes, I know You don't give us the spirit of fear, but today it's there. I don't know how to shake it off and keep going. It's what I don't know that frightens me. I ask that You stir up Your boldness within me. Help me put on Your whole armor. I can't move without it, and frankly, I never want to. I know wherever You are, there is light for me to see my way through.

Amen

Prayer

Date: _____

_____

_____

_____

_____

_____

_____

_____

_____

_____

_____

_____

_____

_____

_____

_____

_____

_____

_____

_____

_____

_____

_____

Dear Lord,

I am numb. The way I see it is if I am numb, I won't have to feel the hurt, the pain, the lies, or deceit anymore than I have to. I seek time to heal; to unplug from everyone and plug into You and You alone. Sometimes, it's hard to realize that You are the only power source I need. You are more than enough. Your cup is the only one that can be forever filled AND with a constant overflow. I am constantly trying to drink from a dry well. I constantly depend on man, and it's never enough. Allow me to drink from Your well. The only one that never runs dry.

Amen

Prayer

Date: _____

Dear Lord,

Whatever You are doing in this season, PLEASE don't do it without me. Keep Your hands on me and my family at all times. I am not worthy, and I am so glad You do things because of who You are not based on who I am. All I have to offer is a HALLELUJAH praise. I will sing it as high as the sky will go. I will sing it when I'm deep in the valley. Continue to keep me in Your will and Your way. I can't do this by myself, and truth be told, I don't want to.

Amen

Prayer

Date: _____

_____
_____
_____
_____
_____
_____
_____
_____
_____
_____
_____
_____
_____
_____
_____
_____
_____
_____
_____
_____
_____
_____
_____
_____
_____

Dear Lord,

I seek wisdom. No more do I want to be blind to the things that are supposed to make me better. No longer do I want peripheral vision. No longer do I want my ideas or my visions. No more seeing from my perspective or leaning to my own understanding. Bless me to see from Your point of view. I want to grow in You, Lord, daily. The way I perceive things makes me worried, frustrated, and sad. I know wisdom from Your well is positive. There will be no confusion. It will send a powerful praise to Your name. Wisdom from You, God will ease my mind and heart. It will birth a new vision from You. I will see all the good in every situation. It all will make sense.

Amen

Prayer

Date: _____

Dear Lord,

On the days I can't seem to find the words, please allow me to just rest in Your arms and listen to every one of my heartbeats. Every beat has a meaning that only You can understand. Comfort me. Allow me to feel ALL of You as I become centered back in Your peace. Father God, I thank You as I know the fear will fade and my faith will be restored. The more intimate I become with You, the more ease and relaxation I'll feel. As You continually come to my rescue over and over again I say THANK YOU. My everlasting, my first resort, my understanding, my God.

Amen

Prayer

Date: _____

Dear Lord,

I thank You for NEW miracles of today! As I go about my day I ask that You show me YOU everywhere I go. Open my eyes to see all of Your goodness that I've been blinded by. Let me see Your goodness that I've taken for granted as if it was an entitlement, and not a BLESSING. Allow my ears to hear Your Word, a special Word from You. Lord, I yearn for ALL of You daily. To see, to hear, to feel the love, joy, and peace that You endlessly shower me with. Anoint my walk and my talk to be lived as the life You've created me to live. Father keep me close to You, ALWAYS. Please don't ever take Your hands off of me or turn Your back on me because without You I AM NOTHING. I'll always need You. Even on days I may forget I need You.

Amen

Prayer

Date: _____

_____
_____
_____
_____
_____
_____
_____
_____
_____
_____
_____
_____
_____
_____
_____
_____
_____
_____
_____
_____
_____
_____
_____
_____
_____
_____

Dear Lord,

Always protect me from the people and things whose purpose is to cause harm to my life. If it's not to bring me closer to You, I ask for blockage right now IN JESUS' NAME. You said the weapons may form, BUT THEY WON'T PROSPER. And Lord I am standing ten toes down on Your Word. The attacks of the enemy, I rebuke them right now in The Mighty Name of JESUS. Any disease and attacks on my body, mind, and soul I give them to You because You are the Only One who can destroy them forever! Keep me covered from the things I can and can't see as I do my walk of life. Lord, I can't do this by myself, and Lord, I don't want to. I pray for discernment. Please don't allow me to be blindsided by anything not sent by You. As long as You are my protector, my Jehova Nissi, I am assured that everything will be well, especially when I fight against any blockage You put up for me. Lord, PROTECT me even from myself. I desire all of You, and none of me. Being only human, I know I need Your constant grace and mercy. As I walk through my Red Sea, drown the things that try to pull me back, hinder me, or trip me. I TRUST YOU GOD.

Amen

Prayer

Date: _____

_____
_____
_____
_____
_____
_____
_____
_____
_____
_____
_____
_____
_____
_____
_____
_____
_____
_____
_____
_____
_____
_____
_____

Dear Lord,

Heal the little girl deep within me. Heal her from all her past hurts and traumas. Heal her mind of all the negative thoughts that have the future her doubting who You created her to be. Whatever was broken, I'm asking for restoration above and beyond what she can even imagine. Anytime those things try to come back and disrupt her mind, build walls and fences all around her. When those unfriendly memories creep in, show her the future ME so I can begin to LIVE the life You want me to live. Help me to walk the path You paved just for me and live my purposeful life. Father, I ask for understanding of it all when the time is right. When I am able to handle TRUTH, reveal what needs to be revealed. I know that You do everything with purpose. Teach me to accept that, and to be thankful for it, even for the unknown and confusing. Lord, I want to be at the point of trusting You COMPLETELY. I THANK YOU my Jehovah Rapha. I rejoice out loud because I know You are always on time, and when You show up, YOU SHOW OUT!

Amen

Prayer

Date: _____

Dear Lord,

I know I'm always asking, asking, asking. Well, today I just want to THANK YOU, THANK YOU, THANK YOU!! For the things I acknowledge, and especially for the things I don't, I THANK YOU. For the things I take for granted, I THANK YOU, Lord. Living, breathing without machines, the activity of my limbs, closed in my right mind, eyes to see, ears to hear, for it ALL, I THANK YOU. I owe it all to You, and You definitely deserve my HALLELUJAH praise. For You being here, being consistent, being my unconditional LOVING GOD, I THANK YOU. The times You have held me close, carrying me through storms, lighting my darkest paths, I glorify Your name. God, You have never given up on me or turned Your back on me. For that, I am eternally grateful. Having all the patience in the world with me, showing new grace and new mercy EVERY DAY. Father, I THANK YOU. You are worthy to be praised in all my goings and comings.

Amen

Prayer

Date: _____

_____
_____
_____
_____
_____
_____
_____
_____
_____
_____
_____
_____
_____
_____
_____
_____
_____
_____
_____
_____
_____
_____
_____

Dear Lord,

Show me, ME; the way You see me, and the way I'm supposed to see myself. Show me the Woman of God that roars deep down inside of me. Allow her to burst out into fullness. My beauty, my confidence, my truth, my worth... allow it all to be seen. I want my posture to rise up in boldness that I AM who God says I AM, and that I will be who God has called me to be. All the doubt, all the fear, all the voices, I rebuke them right now in the name of JESUS. I want more of You, less of me. Lord, I need Your strength and power to be the BEST ME I was created to be.

Amen

Prayer

Date: _____

_____
_____
_____
_____
_____
_____
_____
_____
_____
_____
_____
_____
_____
_____
_____
_____
_____
_____
_____
_____
_____
_____
_____
_____
_____
_____
_____

Dear Lord,

Thank You for being my Friend. For being my Mother and Father on those extra lonely days. You are my go-to for my highs, lows, and in-between. You are my perfect person and Leader. Mold me to be like You; so humble, so kind, so giving, and so trustworthy. Shape humbleness within me. Don't ever let me get big-headed and forget YOU. Always remind me that I need You. Jesus had so much power yet He still SERVED. His humbleness is inspiring, and I want to be more and more like Him. I want to live my life to please You and only You, to do Your will and your way. When people cross my path, I want them to be able to see You and Your goodness.

Amen

Prayer

Date: _____

_____

_____

_____

_____

_____

_____

_____

_____

_____

_____

_____

_____

_____

_____

_____

_____

_____

_____

_____

_____

_____

_____

_____

Dear Lord,

I pray for my PEACE over all situations. No matter what trials and tribulations come my way, my peace will remain. I recognize there isn't anything happening that You didn't permit. I desire a greater level of peace that says GLORY BE TO GOD everything will be okay no matter what I am facing. Help me to keep my peace when You want me to hold on, and my peace when You want me to let go. As the storms rage all around me I'll still have my PEACE. Give me the mindset that nothing in this world can disrupt my peace. As You give it to me instill it in me that ONLY YOU can take it away from me. Lord, I am so thankful that You are my Jehovah Shalom.

Amen

Prayer

Date: _____

Dear Lord,

While You are teaching me, help me to ACCEPT Your teachings. When my flesh wants to be disobedient, keep me on Your straight and narrow. I need Your help always because it has been proven plenty that I can't do anything without YOU. Truth be told I don't want to! Help me to trust You and Your Word at all times. When the teachings become challenging and my flesh weakens, as it may want to seek revenge, Lord God, PLEASE INTERVENE. Don't let me fall victim once again. I want to be victorious in JESUS' NAME. I want to walk into "LOOK AT WHAT GOD DID IN ME, AGAIN." I always ask You to protect me from others, but I need You to protect me from myself as well. I am just as human as the next. Your guidance will always be needed.

Amen

Prayer

Date: _____

Dear Lord,

Position me right where You want me to be at this very moment. If I attempt to step out of Your light, position me back immediately. I'll admit sometimes old habits tug and pull at me to return to a familiar, but I do not want that lifestyle anymore. With my growth came wisdom. I was young and dumb. I've grown mentally and spiritually, but I'm not naive to my weak flesh. Every day I have to pick up my cross. Every day I have to die to self. Some days are harder than others, but I know every day, YOU ARE GOD!

Amen

Prayer

Date: _____

Dear Lord,

Thank You for closing doors that I was not strong enough to close on my own. No matter how much I may try to open them, keep them bolted shut. Ignore my tantrums because You and I both know You know what's best for me. Only allow me to walk through doors of prosperity.

Amen

Prayer

Date: _____

_____
_____
_____
_____
_____
_____
_____
_____
_____
_____
_____
_____
_____
_____
_____
_____
_____
_____
_____
_____
_____
_____
_____
_____

Dear Lord,

For my new house, I TRUST YOU, GOD. For my children, I TRUST YOU GOD. For my financial increase, I TRUST YOU, GOD. For my wisdom, peace, joy, and happiness, I TRUST YOU, GOD. For my future, I TRUST YOU, GOD. For the fulfillment of my purpose, I TRUST YOU, GOD. For my healing and deliverance, I TRUST YOU, GOD. For my unknown and the things I can't see, I TRUST YOU, GOD!

Amen

Prayer

Date: _____

Dear Lord,

I want to trust the beauty of Your timing, teach me how to wait. Help me to understand, accept, and LOVE the process of Your timing. Anoint my mind to be delightful in the process. To be joyful that it hasn't happened yet, but You are still working it out for my good. I need timing to dwell in my spirit that timing IS EVERYTHING. Lord, You were in no hurry to create this beautiful world one precious step at a time. And when You were done, You said it was GOOD! This reassures me that as You take Your time and work, a beautiful masterpiece will be made. No mistakes will be made, no half-stepping, no second guessing.

Amen

Prayer

Date: _____

_____
_____
_____
_____
_____
_____
_____
_____
_____
_____
_____
_____
_____
_____
_____
_____
_____
_____
_____
_____
_____
_____
_____
_____

Dear Lord,

I don't always recognize when You don't allow certain things or people to enter into my life. From my perspective I'm sad and I'm confused thinking they should be there; not realizing the GLORY of Your protection over my pathway. As I grow in You, it becomes more and more clear why You say Your ways are not my ways neither Your thoughts my thoughts. I should trust You always! And even though You don't owe me an explanation as to anything you do or don't do, I thank you for sending your soldiers and your perfect timing to answer my wives. Therefore, transferring my whys into thank you Lord for protecting me. Thank you, Lord, for knowing what's best for me. Thank you, Lord, that You and You alone are The Only God who knows my future. You know the who's and the what's that will hurt me. Because of your teachings, my outlook on things is different. I see more positives than negatives now. And in due time I'm speaking THANKS for the moments I'm stepping into and counting it all JOY, in Jesus' name.

Amen

Prayer

Date: _____

_____
_____
_____
_____
_____
_____
_____
_____
_____
_____
_____
_____
_____
_____
_____
_____
_____
_____
_____
_____
_____
_____
_____
_____
_____

Dear Lord,

Anytime someone offends me, hurts my feelings, or says inappropriate things to me, I ask that You correct them, Lord. Correct them every single time Father until you say I am ready to handle the situation. And when it is my time, Lord, anoint my every word that I may receive the correct and respectful way. God, purify my words, tone, posture, attitud,, and everything else that may take offense. Teach me to respond in love and not hate in Jesus' name.

Amen

Prayer

Date: _____

Dear Lord,

Today I pray for my clarity. Lately I've been so confused about so much going on in my life. Today, Father God, I just want clarity. I AM expecting to see You as I've never seen before, and I AM expecting to hear You as I've never heard You before. Just for TODAY, Lord. Please bring clarification on all the things I have been praying to You about. So much doesn't make sense, and I know that it is not You, because You are NOT a God of confusion. That's how I know I need more than usual of You TODAY! Remove, block, or rebuke that which is not of You so I can see, feel, hear, and KNOW You clearly. Lord, I am tired so I really need YOU TODAY in a mighty and special way. Allow Your answers (today) to hit my soul in an unquestionable way. Shower Your answers from the top of my head to the souls of my feet. Let Your answers hit me like a breath of fresh air. When I breathe in, let me hear from You. When I breathe out, let me hear from You. Anything I may read, anyone I may come across, speak directly to me, PLEASE GOD! I need YOU MIGHTILY TODAY.

Amen

Prayer

Date: _____

ABOUT THE AUTHOR

Hi, my name is Samantha NaCole. I am a Woman after God's own heart. I was born in Shallotte, NC, and raised in Ash, NC. I have 4 wonderful blessings who call me Mom. I am a Cosmetologist who specializes in braids of different sorts. I serve on the media team at church, which I love. In my free time, I enjoy spending it with children and writing. One of God's gifts to me is the use of my hands.

www.ingramcontent.com/pod-product-compliance
Lightning Source LLC
Chambersburg PA
CBHW051240120626
46547CB00014B/1723